A Day in the Life of the Maya: History, Cultu ... the Mayan Empire

By Charles River Editors

About Charles River Editors

Charles River Editors was founded by Harvard and MIT alumni to provide superior editing and original writing services, with the expertise to create digital content for publishers across a vast range of subject matter. In addition to providing original digital content for third party publishers, Charles River Editors republishes civilization's greatest literary works, bringing them to a new generation via ebooks.

Introduction

Mayapan

"More than a collection of quaint mythology and exotic rituals, [Maya] religion was an effective definition of the nature of the world, answering questions about the origin of humanity, the purpose of human life on earth, and the relationship of the individual to his family, his society, and his gods. It is a religion which speaks to central and enduring problems of the civilized human condition: power, justice, equality, individual purpose, and social destiny." - *A Forest of Kings: The Untold Story of the Ancient Maya*

Many ancient civilizations have influenced and inspired people in the 21st century. The Greeks and Romans continue to fascinate the West today. But of all the world's civilizations, none have intrigued people more than the Mayans, whose culture, astronomy, language, and mysterious disappearance all continue to captivate people. In 2012 especially, there has been a renewed focus on the Mayans, whose advanced calendar has led many to speculate the world will end on the same date the Mayan calendar ends. The focus on the "doomsday" scenario, however, has overshadowed the Mayans' true contribution to astronomy, language, sports, and art.

The Maya are one of the most famous civilizations in history, but what was it like to be Mayan at the height of their civilization in the 15th century? What were their settlements like, what did they eat, how did they play, how did they fight, and what did they believe in? *A Day in the Life of the Maya* answers these questions by comprehensively examining and analyzing everything about their culture, including their history, religion, architecture, farming, calendar, ball game, cosmology and origins. Along with a description of Mayan life and pictures of Mayan ruins and art, the mystique of the Maya is traced from the height of their empire to the present day, in an attempt to understand a civilization often been best described as an enigma.

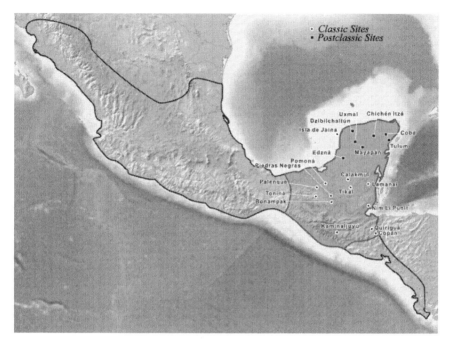

Map of the Mayan Empire

Chapter 1: The Enigma of the Maya

Depiction of Upakal K'inich in Palenque

Ubiquitous in popular and scholarly descriptions of Maya civilization is the word enigma. In spite of tremendous advances in archaeology that continue to reveal more and more information on the highly developed Maya civilization of Mesoamerica, there remain many unanswered questions. Two examples of significant unresolved questions concerning the Maya illustrate the serious holes in our knowledge. Despite the existence of their civilization in South America for thousands of years, historians and archaeologists still cannot explain where the Maya came from or exactly why their civilization collapsed.

Why have these questions continued to go unanswered? These unsolved mysteries surrounding the Maya civilization persist in large measure due to the efficiency of the Spanish in eradicating the remnants of Maya culture. And unlike the Aztecs, the disappearance of the Mayans cannot be clearly traced to a series of battles. By the early 16th century the Spanish conquistadors, along with the colonists and zealous propagators of the faith who followed the likes of Cortes and Pizarro, set out to systematically destroy the indigenous Maya civilization of the Yucatan that was already in decline even before their arrival. The land-grabbing colonists used the natives as virtual slave labor and pillaged their cities, while enthusiastic Catholic baptizers did their best to erase their heathen beliefs.

While the blame for the loss of much of the Mayan culture can be heaped upon the Spanish, much of what is known about life in a Maya community comes from the writings of the Provincial of the Franciscans in the Yucatan, Bishop Diego de Landa. His 1566 book, *Relación de las cosas de Yucatán* (An Account of the Affairs in the Yucatan), contains detailed observations on the culture of the Maya, including a record of their hieroglyphics and writing system. These have proved to be invaluable sources for those piecing together a picture of Mayan life. But Bishop Landa was also responsible for what in retrospect was an incalculable loss for the world. The Mayans' developed the only full language during the Mesoamerican period, but Landa and his Franciscan cohorts confiscated a great number of books written in the Mayan language which they believed were full of heretical ideas and burned them all. Bishop Landa's well-intentioned bonfire of books left the world with only four extant Maya manuscripts and a 1558 record written in Latin characters of Maya cosmology called the *Popol Vuh*, or book of the people preserving oral tradition of the K'iche Maya of Guatemala.

The Maya's writings obviously weren't the only things lost to history. In the years after the conquest of the Maya some of their cities were mined by the colonists for building materials. A spectacular example of this is took place at Izamal, where Bishop Landa's Monastery of San Antonio de Padua was constructed with stones reused from a Maya building. The Monastery itself, rising above the colonial town, sits on a plinth that is, in fact, a truncated Maya pyramid. Other Maya cities still inhabited in the period of conquest were abandoned and eventually obscured by jungle vegetation. Explorers in the jungle still find lost ruins of the Maya in Central America, and one incorrect story that made the rounds in 2011 speculated that Mayan ruins were found in North Georgia, a reflection of the interest and uncertainty still surrounding the Maya.

In the early 19th century, explorers and adventurers began to rediscover several Maya sites. Following the opinions of the colonists, who at the time perceived the contemporary Maya as unsophisticated and culturally impoverished, the explorers were initially convinced that these people could not have been responsible for such elaborate building projects. Given some of their similarities to the ancient civilizations in Europe and Egypt, they concluded that the Maya pyramids and other structures they discovered must have somehow been the work of Greeks, Romans, Egyptians or Indians from India. How exactly these American city builders got to the region was explained by fanciful conjecture on cultural migration.

In the middle of the 19th century, John Lloyd Stephens and the topographical artist Frederick

Catherwood systematically explored the Mayan ruins of British Honduras, Guatemala and the Yucatan. The subsequent publication of Stephens' description of the Maya ruins and Catherwood's illustrations in *Incidents of Travel in Central America, Chiapas, and the Yucatán* in 1841 and *Incidents of Travel in Yucatán* in 1843 were best sellers. They were also responsible for an upsurge in interest in the mysteries of lost civilizations. In the last half of the 19th century, a number of other explorers recorded Maya sites, and in 1881, English archaeologist Alfred Maudslay began the first modern scientific study of a number of Maya cities. His work inspired American archaeologists associated with Harvard University to undertake expeditions, and these in turn were followed by many university and museum sponsored digs right up to the present day. Interest in the Maya began an upswing that carries through today.

The many (and ongoing) accounts of discoveries of Mayan cities by archaeologists and explorers have only added to the mysteries of the Maya civilization, which in turn continue to fuel interest and speculation. Early archaeologists attributed names to the buildings in many sites based on assumptions as to their use, which has led to misleading descriptions that should be paid little attention. At Uxmal, today a very popular Yucatan tourist destination, there are buildings called the Nunnery and the Governor's Palace, both of which are based on quite fanciful ideas of the original purpose of the structures. At Chichén Itzá, the greatest Maya city in the Yucatan, one is taken by guides to a building called the Nunnery for no good reason other than the small rooms reminded the Spaniards of a nunnery back home. Similarly the great pyramid at Chichén Itzá is designated the El Castillo, the Castle, which it certainly is not, and the Observatory is called El Caracol, the Snail, for its spiral staircase. This kind of confusing naming of Maya structures had been abandoned at recently discovered sites and replaced with less colorful terms such as, for example, Temple 1, Temple II and so on at Tikal in Guatemala.

The Pyramid of the Magician at Uxmal and Building of the Iguana at Uxmal are perfect examples of fanciful but nonsensical names

The Castle at Chichén Itzá

Chapter 2: The Origins and Spreading of the Maya Civilization

Today the Aztecs are remembered as the civilization with the vast South American empire, but the Mayans spread across a wide swath of land themselves. The region of Mesoamerica inhabited by the Maya stretched from the dry, flat limestone plains of the Yucatan to the wet, mountainous jungle of Chiapas and Guatemala and on to the narrow flatland of the Pacific coast. The first inhabitants of the region are believed to have been hunter gatherers, and anthropologists think these primitive people were descended from the early migrants who moved from Asia across to the northern reaches of North America and spread south around 14,000 B.C. Once settled, a more agricultural society developed in central Mexico in the fifth millennium BCE. These people were able to reliably grow crops of corn, beans and squashes through slash and burn field preparation, but depending on the quantity and quality of the soil, a field had a limited life expectancy. In some regions, particularly those where the soil cover was thin and the rainfall limited, the slash and burn technique of crop cultivation required careful attention to the seasonal weather pattern.

Around 1800 B.C., the Olmecs, the earliest traceable civilization of Mesoamerica, built cities that depended on reliable agricultural production. Many details of Olmec society remain a mystery, but it is known that some of their practices, such as building pyramids and playing a ritual ball-game, were similar to those of the later Maya. Nevertheless, the precise relationship between the Olmec and the Maya culture is as yet unknown. What is known is that while the earliest Maya communities on the Pacific coast and in the Guatemalan highlands and Belize were on the rise, the Olmec civilization, with its population centers near the region of modern Veracruz and Villahermosa in Mexico, was in decline.

The history of the Maya is divided into periods that have been given names and dates that are not currently unanimously accepted. The nomenclature of the chronology of Maya civilization was created by Eurocentric scholars who held fixed ideas on the rise, flourishing and decline of civilizations, in keeping with the tracking of the Greek and Roman empires of antiquity. In particular, readers should be cautious of the word classic, as it implies a superior rank or model or standard which does not really apply to the evolution of Maya culture. Still, this chronology, even with its imperfections, does allow for a quick survey of the evolution of Maya civilization.

The Early Preclassic period dating from 1800 to 900 B.C. is the era when the Olmecs established their major cities at Paso de la Amada in Chiapas and San Lorenzo in southern Veracruz. In the Middle Preclassic Period, spanning the years from 900 to 300 B.C., the first Maya cities were built on the Pacific coast, in places like Itzapa near Tapachula, in the Guatemalan highlands at such sites as Kaminaljuyú now underneath Guatemala City, and the recently excavated mega-city El Mirador. It is currently held that Maya city building expanded north further into the Guatemalan Highlands and Belize.

Pyramid at El Mirador

It was in the Late Preclassic Period from 300 B.C.-250 A.D. that archaeologists believe Maya culture developed a high level of complexity. This included the appearance of writing in the Mayan language and a sophisticated continuing calendar system. In the Early Classic Period, 250-600 A.D., Maya civilization flourished, particularly in the city of Tikal in modern Guatemala. Major construction was carried out at Copán in modern Honduras and at Palenque in Chiapas, Mexico. The period Late Classic, 600-950 A.D., is used by Mayanists to designate the age in which civilization reached its height. This was the time when the great cities of the Yucatan or northern lowlands flourished and the cities of the southern lowlands declined. It was also late in this period that the city of Chichén Itzá rose to prominence.

The Main Plaza at Tikal

The final period in the chronology used by scholars of Maya civilization is the Post Classic Period 950-1530 A.D. which saw the collapse of Chichén Itzá and the rise of Mayapán, the last leading city of Maya culture. The four surviving Mayan codices were written during this period.

Given the manner in which Maya cities flourished in different periods and were built in different environments, from the lush jungle in the south to the wet coastlands of Belize and the dry limestone plains of the Yucatan, it is not surprising that the Maya were not a homogenous people. In different regions of their empire, Mayan people and cities had distinctly different economies, social organization, art and architecture. Variation existed over time and geography. It is important to keep that in mind when discussing Mayan culture.

Chapter 3: Life in a Maya City

Social Status

Mayan panel depicting King T'ah 'Ak' Cha'an

Maya civic society in its fully developed form was organized around a king or *ahau*, from whose lineage his successors were chosen. The king or lord was the embodiment of religious life in the city, and for that he was assisted by noble warriors, the *sahalob*. The Maya believed that the well-being of the rest of the community depended on the religious rituals performed by the royal court, so the community supported the *ahau* and his clan with voluntary offerings of food and labor. The former would have been particularly burdensome in years of drought in the northern lowlands, and the latter must have been exceedingly taxing considering how much stone and rubble was transported in the process of building pyramids, palaces, temples and roads.

Not every contribution was voluntary, however. The king not only received levies from the inhabitants of his city, but he also, in some cases, required that vassal cities and communities render him tribute. The wealth of a king and his court was thus directly dependent on how many vassal states he had and the population of his own city. The king and his clan of aristocrats consequently lived better than everyone else and enjoyed an abundance of luxuries provided as tribute or through trading the excess of this "in kind" payment with neighboring cities. In this way jade, amber and obsidian, cotton, cacao, honey and salt were available to the principal kings and their courts.

Based on depictions in sculpture and wall paintings in the Classic Period, the Maya kings, presumably only on formal occasions, sported large headdresses that were held up by racks attached to their backs. These wooden decorations were painted and enriched with shells, jade, feathers and textiles and sometimes an image of Chaac, the rain god, or Ahau Kin, the sun god. The nose, which was a particularly important element in the Maya concept of beauty, would be built up with putty. To obtain a nose with a profile that was a continuation of the slope of the forehead, aristocratic Mayans bound an infant's head with a board to control its shape. The ears of the kings and aristocrats were decorated with elaborate ornaments attached to enlarged lobes, and their teeth were carefully filed and filled with inlays of jade. The king had a wardrobe of formal costumes so that he appeared in garb appropriate to his functions as priest, war lord, or presiding official at ball games.

The power and central importance of a king in Maya culture is illustrated in the impressive memorial structure built by King Pakal at Palenque in Mexico. Several years before his death at the age of 81 in 684 A.D. Pakal had a 27 meter pyramid constructed against a natural hill. His nine level pyramid with a steep narrow stairway running up the front is topped by a temple with five entrances. On the pillars between the entrances are inscriptions recording the royal lineage of Pakal. From the Temple of Inscriptions, a stairway leads down into the bowels of the pyramid to a burial crypt. Here King Pakal's body, decorated with jade necklaces and wearing a face mask of jade obsidian and shells, was entombed in a painted sarcophagus. On the lid of the sarcophagus was carved an image of Pakal descending the world-tree into the underworld. When the crypt was discovered in 1951, it contained the skeletons of four malew and one female. It is assumed that the bones are the remains of captives sacrificed to accompany Pakal to the underworld.

King Pakal himself began the building of his tomb. It was completed during the reign of his son Kan-Balam II who recorded his contribution by having a stucco panel installed in the Temple of Inscriptions showing him as a baby in his father's arms.

The society of the Maya was stratified. The king who owed his position to a royal lineage was surrounded by nobles that obtained their rank through paternal descent, although their status was even higher if they were also descended from nobility on the maternal side. Among the nobility in some Maya cities were prosperous farmers, successful merchants, priests and warriors. The duties of the court included maintaining civic order, recording the history of the community in sculpture and inscriptions, keeping the calendar, recording astronomical information and divining the future from it, and managing war and trade. Below the nobility were the free workers who were allocated a *hun* or *uinic* of 400 square feet of land to farm. They paid an in-kind levy to the king and temple priests, who would divine ideal times for planting and harvest. The Mayans strongly that neither good things nor bad things occurred by chance, which is why they were so bent on studying the patterns of the sun and stars. They believed these patterns were set in motion by the gods to help the Maya reveal their divine intentions.

In addition to Maya inscriptions and sculpture that have now been deciphered, information on life in a Maya city was recorded by Bishop Diego de Landa in his *Relación*. As a Christian European, he was fascinated with the Maya system of justice. In particular, he recorded the various crimes that involved a punishment of execution and public humiliation. One of the details he included in his account was the punishment for adultery. The guilty party would be punished by having his head crushed by a rock thrown by the offended husband. For lesser crimes such as theft, the culprit was put into temporary slavery. This would be humiliating to the Mayans, because the permanent slaves in a typical Maya community were low level captives of war. The more prestigious captives of war were "luckier." These prestigious enemy warriors were spared a life of slavery and were apparently treated well until they were required for ritual sacrifice.

Food and Farming

The vast majority of the population of Maya cities consisted of farmers, who mostly lived in wood-framed reed huts on an elevated platform, much like those that can be seen today in rural Mayan communities in the Yucatan. This was sensible, since a high level of food production was necessary to sustain populations that were quite astonishing in size. In the Late Classic period around 600 A.D., the city of Tikal in Guatemala is estimated to have had a population of 39,000 people, with another 10,000 living in the hinterland around the city. At its peak, Palenque had about 6,000 inhabitants, Uxmal had perhaps 15,000, and Chichén Itzá may have had over 30,000 inhabitants. With different features and climates, the methods and successes of farming around these various communities were not always similar. In the northern lowlands, cities such as Uxmal and Chichén Itzá had precarious food supplies that depended, in part, on slash and burn agriculture. In the farthest reaches of the southern lowlands, at cities like Palenque, water was plentiful and reliable crop production was the norm. Here, because the depth of the soil was significantly more than that of the northern lowlands, cleared land could be productive for 10 years or longer.

Mayan farms produced a variety of crops, the staples being corn or maize with beans and squashes. In some Maya communities, cotton, cocoa and honey were produced, and whatever wasn't used for basic living was traded. Along the coast of modern Belize, Maya agricultural practices included the use of irrigation ditches, mounded fields and reclamation of swamp land. These techniques would have ensured a very long period of productivity for agriculture.

Depending on the location of their community, the Mayans typically ate animals that they hunted, and along the shore in the Yucatan at maritime trading cities like Cozumel and Tulum, and in Belize, the Maya had a diet that included quantities of fish.

Warfare

It is a commonly held belief among scholars that warfare between Maya cities erupted when there was a shortage of food, either because of drought or insufficient production to support an expanding population. Although there is no direct evidence, it is supposed that one city would expand into the territory of another and there would be competition for land.

Most of the theories on Maya warfare are based on two fairly inadequate assumptions. One is that all Maya city populations were identical over the entire history of the civilization, and the other is that Maya behaved like Europeans. Instead, some scholars now believe that some Maya cities engaged in ferocious warfare from time to time, while others were involved in only occasional skirmishes with their neighbors. In piecing together the evidence of Maya culture it is necessary to remember that the Maya civilization of interest to archaeologists existed between 900 B.C.-1200 A.D., and that their cities were scattered in the huge territory lying between the Pacific coast of Guatemala and the northern reaches of the Yucatan peninsula. To assume that Maya culture was monolithic and consistent is a holdover from colonial beliefs in the simplicity of the indigenous people they conquered.

While it has historically been the Aztecs who were viewed as a militaristic civilization, there is considerable debate among scholars on the question of territorial aggression among the Maya. Because many of the Maya cities lack fortifications that are like those Eurocentric archaeologists might have expected, it was once assumed that the Maya created for themselves an ideal, pacifistic society. But others have considered the Maya as particularly ferocious in warfare, taking captives for ritual sacrifice and appropriating territories through force. Still others have explained the demise of certain Maya cities by arguing that they were devastated by internecine warfare that doomed both sides of the fighting. As with many aspects of Maya society, the presence or absence of bellicose behavior is an enigma. There have been some findings of parapets and ramparts, in particular at Tikal and Becán, clear proof that the Mayans saw the need for defensive fortifications for those cities. But the fact that such ramparts were not a consistent part of Maya city construction is evidence that there was considerable variation in aggression, expansion and cooperation from one city to another.

Chapter 4: Cities of the Maya

The Maya had a unique urban culture that is evident from both the remains of their earliest settlements in the highlands of Guatemala and the last of the great Maya cities, Mayapán in the Yucatan. The planning of Maya cities, the arrangement of buildings in the center, and the disposition of small farms and dwellings forming the urban area remained generally consistent throughout the centuries, regardless of the different developments of their culture.

The first great Maya city that has been discovered is the recently excavated El Mirador in Guatemala. Archaeologists believe that it flourished between 200 B.C.-150 A.D. and had a population in the tens of thousands spread over nearly 10 square miles. As was common among the Maya, part of the city of El Mirador is built on the foundations of prior construction dating from the Middle Preclassic Period. The central east-west axis of the city joins two massive complexes separated by over a mile. At one end the tallest Maya pyramid rising over 200 feet dominates a plaza and two lateral temples. On the lower levels of these temples, archaeologists unearthed stucco jaguar masks, and adjacent to these temples is a burial acropolis which held the bodies of priests and noblemen surrounded by obsidian lancets and stingray spines. These tools were used to pierce the penis, ears and tongue in bloodletting rituals that were common in all great Maya cities. Bloodletting was a means to invoke the gods and ensure their presence in the Mayans' lives. On the other end of the city axis at El Mirador, a slightly lower pyramid is flanked by two temples. The size and complexity of the city of El Mirador makes clear that even during the so-called Preclassic Era, the Maya civilization had reached a particularly high level of architectural, artistic and social sophistication.

The Temple at Tikal

The city of Tikal, also in the Guatemalan highland rainforest, is an example of a Classic Maya city. At the site of Tikal a modest village was established perhaps as early as 900 B.C., and as archaeological evidence suggests, some 400 years later the population had expanded to a level sufficient for the construction of a small astronomical temple. After 250 B.C., the first ceremonial buildings were erected, including a pyramid and modest temples. The Great Plaza of Tikal begun around the beginning of the Common Era was followed by massive construction that stretched over the next 200 years. This increasingly elaborate architecture and decoration formed the basis for re-building and expansion of the ceremonial precincts in the classic period from 400 to 909 CE, when Tikal reached the zenith of its power even though it suffered from unsuccessful wars with Caracol in modern Belize. A great deal is known about the dynastic history of Tikal and its various wars and alliances with neighboring cities. One King Hasaw Chan K'awil waged a successful campaign in 696 against the city of Calakmul which had at one point overrun Tikal. In a period of peace Hasaw Chan K'awil's son Yik'in Chan K'awil launched a building campaign creating five of Tikal's most important temples. In one of them he entombed his father's body. Around the year 900 Tikal collapsed and was abandoned.

Uxmal

In the Late Classic Period, from 600-950 A.D., the Maya cities of the Yucatan flourished. The best known of these are a cluster of sites in the Puuc hills south of the modern city of Mérida.

The most elaborate and finest of Maya architecture is found here cities like Uxmal, Sayil and Kabah. At Uxmal, the *ahau* or king, known as Lord Chak (c. 890-910), was responsible for the construction of several of the major structures, including what is known as the Nunnery and the Governor's Palace. The decoration of these building with intricate relief carvings on inset flat and bowed stones, and the use of three dimensional mosaic patterns in the masonry, represents the zenith of the Mayans' architectural finesse.

The cities of the Puuc hills seem to have had a peaceful cooperative relationship with each other. Roads with cut stone curbs connected them together, and one of the roads that ran from Kabah to Uxmal was decorated with the largest extant Maya monumental corbelled arch. The Maya did not have in their repertoire of architectural forms an arch with a keystone, rather they used the corbelled arch in which from the springing of the arch stones in successive courses are offset. The corbelled arch required massive amounts of masonry to ensure stability and had a limited span, so arched interior rooms in Maya temples and other structures are long and narrow.

Arch over the road from Kabah to Uxmal, Kabah (Photo: Alan McNairn)

The most visited and the most spectacular of Late Classic Maya cities is Chichén Itzá, which was very large and became a very influential center in the later years of Maya civilization. With a spectacular pyramid, enormous ball court, observatory and several temples, the builders of this city exceeded even those at Uxmal in developing the use of columns and exterior relief decoration. Of particular interest at Chichén Itzá is the sacred cenote, which is accessed by a road from the central plaza. The cenote or sinkhole was a focus for Maya rituals around water. Because adequate supplies of water, which rarely collected on the surface of the limestone based

Yucatan, were essential for adequate agricultural production, the Maya here considered it of primary importance. Underwater archaeology carried out in the cenote at Chichén Itzá revealed that offerings to the Maya rain deity Chaac (which may have included people) were tossed into the sinkhole. Chichén Itzá had a relatively short period of dominance in the region, lasting from about 800-950 A.D.

Ruins at Chichén Itzá

El Castillo or Pyramid, Chichén Itzá

The last city of the Maya to rise to prominence was Mayapán in the Yucatan. Its glory days were around 1200 CE, and it collapsed just before the arrival of the Spanish. The finish and decoration of the buildings in this city are considered to be significantly less accomplished than those in the earlier Maya communities, because the builders apparently used less than exacting standards. This approach to the archaeological evidence of Mayapán is based on the long accepted chronology of Maya civilization which placed emphasis on art and architectural achievements of the Classic Period, a designation based on the quality of the elite material culture. Archaeology was at one point an essential supplier of museum exhibits, and up until very recently, museums had very little interest in displaying the mundane everyday objects of a culture. Still, it is important to remember that the supposed decline of architecture and architectural ornament at Mayapán should not be taken as an indicator of the decline of Maya civilization. After all, today's modern cities often involve varying degrees of quality, even in the same city. Certain areas of Queens do not resemble the Upper West Side of Manhattan, but that hardly means New York City is in decline.

Chapter 5: The Popol Vuh

"THIS IS THE BEGINNING of the old traditions of this place called Quiché. Here we shall write and we shall begin the old stories, the beginning and the origin of all that was done in the town of the Quiché, by the tribes of the Quiché nation. And here we shall set forth the revelation, the declaration, and the narration of all that was hidden, the revelation by Tzacol, Bitol, Alom, Qaholom, who are called Hunahpú-Vuch, Hunahpú-Utiú, Zaqui-Nimá-Tziís, Tepeu, Gucumatz, u Qux cho, u Qux Paló, Ali Raxá Lac, Ah Raxá Tzel, as they were called." – Preamble of the *Popol Vuh*

Unlike most Native American civilizations, several Mesoamerican cultures developed true writing systems, led by either the Olmec or the Maya. Recent scholarship has revealed evidence that writing may have been developed first among the Olmec. Between 1400 and 400 B.C., this civilization flourished in the lowlands on the coast of the Gulf of Mexico, in present-day Tabasco and Veracruz, Mexico and may have been where Mesoamerican cultures first developed hieroglyphic writing. However, because they wrote mostly on bark-paper, very few examples of Olmec writing have survived. The Maya, on the other hand, wrote extensively on public structures and monuments, recording important dates such as dates of accession of their *Ahaus*, as the rulers of their city-states were known. Maya scribes also recorded events from religious texts such as *The Popol Vuh* in frescoes painted in ceremonial or funerary locations and complete with hieroglyphics recounting the scene being depicted. Specific events and rituals from Maya religious practice were recorded artistically, often in stone accompanied by a hieroglyphic narrative of the events. Writing served a vital purpose in Maya society by documenting the achievements and lineages of the elite families–who served as the various city-states–and codifying and solidifying aspects of religious belief and practice.

While the Maya perpetuated both oral and written religious traditions, it is the development of a writing system and the transcription of what likely started as oral traditions into written form that allowed the survival of much Maya religious belief and practice. A hieroglyphic writing system might seem ponderous and impractical, especially when one considers that the Maya were a largely urban civilization with a complex and highly stratified class system and coordinating the bureaucratic needs of such detailed systems required easy and quick documentation methods. Also, Maya trade routes extended literally thousands of miles and included peoples from the present-day Caribbean to Columbia and from modern Florida to New Mexico. The writing system existed (like the ball game) at many levels. There are simplified versions of the detailed and ornate glyphs found inscribed on buildings and monuments that allowed rapid transcription of and documentation of information.

Maya hieroglyphic writing was both logographic and phonographic. Each glyph has a word value based on it as a complete whole (its logographic value) and a value based on it as a phonetic word part (its phonographic value). This is depicted in the glyph for the first day of the twenty-day cycle of the Maya calendar, *imix*.

The glyph is a rounded rectangular field with a rough circle or oval centered in the top third. Several versions appear, some with arcing lines passing across the circle and dots are arranged around the bottom of the circle. Considered as a whole, the glyph possesses a logographic value meaning "imix," the first day. But, it also possesses the phonetic value of *ba* and can be used to create other words in combination with other glyphs.

What is known about the beliefs of the Maya comes primarily from the *Popol Vuh*, a compendium of oral tradition among Guatemalan K'iche Maya. This book, written by a Maya in the 18th century, tells the story of the creation of the earth. It is through a synopsis of the creation myth that people today can get a glimpse of some of the major features of Maya society, including their relationship with the land, the importance of family connections, the duality of the gods, and the central role of corn in the life of the Maya.

The importance of Maya hieroglyphic writing to their religious practice is that their creation story and fundamental aspects of both their society and religion, The *Popol Vuh*, was transcribed early during the Spanish conquest and colonial period probably from a hieroglyphic codex of the narrative, giving modern scholars a glimpse into pre-Columbian Maya writing and one of its fundamental purposes. In addition to inscribing monuments, the Maya also produced codex-books, wooden plates covered with bark paper texts and connected accordion-style. After the colonization of Mexico and Guatemala, Catholic missionaries actively collected and destroyed Maya texts. In one episode, Spanish priests burned some 4,000 Maya codices in an attempt to end indigenous religious practices among the Maya, and they often used torture to elicit the locations of books from their Maya victims. Only four Maya codices survived the early Spanish colonial period, while the Aztecs, whose writing system was similar to that of the Maya, fared better in that 16 of their books survived the Catholic conflagration after Cortés's conquest of Tenochtitlan.

The *Popol Vuh* demonstrates a primary difference between Maya writing and modern, European-based writing styles; it presents information out of order and requires careful analysis and familiarity to understand the order of events and keep track of key actors. The narrative likely represents a record designed to be read and delivered to a population who already knew the story, and The *Popol Vuh* represents only the indigenous religious aspect of Maya civilization during the Classic Period, though fundamental aspects of the narrative are nearly a millennium older. This is in contrast to modern times, as today most Maya practice a syncretic blend of Catholicism and indigenous religious practice. In highland Guatemala, Maya religious practice has entered Catholic religious rituals, as shown by the "sawdust carpets" over which Maya Catholics carry statues of saints during the pre-Easter holy week. The carpets are thick sawdust walkways, painted with images and brightly colored, and as the saints are carried over them they are destroyed. This ritual is nearly identical to a Maya religious procession in which the destruction of the brightly painted carpet represents renewal and rebirth. The symbolism of the original Maya ritual fits nearly perfectly with the Christian concept of the resurrection of Christ after three days. Also, the concept of Christ entering the underworld would have been a familiar event to newly converted Maya familiar with The *Popol Vuh*, which involved a series of journeys to the underworld and the various versions of human creation.

The *Popol Vuh* was saved by an unknown Quiché (kee-CHE) Maya nobleman, who during the conquest (between 1554 and 1558 AD) likely transcribed a hieroglyphic copy of the narrative phonetically into Roman text. It is known that he was a noble because he knew how to both read the Maya hieroglyphic writing and write Roman text, and in Maya society scribes were required to be of noble birth (related to the Ahau, or somehow a member of the ruling class). Indeed, *The Popol Vuh*, details the sacred origins of writing and explains the provenance of the Maya "Monkey" god, the patron of writing, dance, and calculating. The unknown nobleman/writer was likely close enough to the elite to both survive and quickly learn Spanish. Additionally, because Santa Cruz del Quiché was conquered by Pedro de Alvarado in 1524, this unknown nobleman may have been one of the original Mestizos who sought to preserve the indigenous part of his religious identity. Had he been fathered by a Spanish conquistador and a Maya woman of royal lineage, early in the conquest period, he would have been between 28-32 years of age during the proposed period when the original text was created.

After its creation, the text was hidden for nearly 200 years, when its existence came to the attention of Francisco Ximénez, a Spanish friar who spoke Quiché. At Chichicastenango, Friar Ximénez copied the Quiché text and wrote a parallel Spanish translation which is currently the oldest surviving copy of the *Popol Vuh*. While the *Popol Vuh*'s provenance might be questioned because the oldest example is essentially a colonial document, Maya Ahaus often inscribed monuments or buildings with sculpture and hieroglyphic writing depicting parts of the narrative and dating to the Classic Period and earlier. As indicated earlier, the *Popol Vuh* presents events out of order, but in order to facilitate a clear understanding of the events presented in the narrative, they will be presented here in chronological order.

The oldest written account of the Popol Vuh, early 18th century by Francisco Ximénez

The *Popol Vuh* first presents the Maya version of creation by relating a series of four incarnations of men made from various materials. Unlike the Christian narrative in Genesis, the Maya creation story starts not in chaos but in a time of great quiet and stillness.

"This is the first account, the first narrative. There was neither man, nor animal, birds, fishes, crabs, trees, stones, caves, ravines, grasses, nor forests; there was only the sky. The surface of the earth had not appeared. There was only the calm sea and the great expanse of the sky. There was nothing brought together, nothing which could make a noise, nor anything which might move, or tremble, or could make noise in the sky. There was nothing standing; only the calm water, the placid sea, alone and tranquil. Nothing existed. There was only immobility and silence in the darkness, in the night. Only the creator, the Maker, Tepeu, Gucumatz, the Forefathers, were in the water surrounded with light. [...] Then Tepeu and Gucumatz came together; then they conferred about life and light, what they would do so that there would be light and dawn, who it would be who would provide food and sustenance. Thus let it be done! Let the emptiness be filled! Let the water recede and make a void, let the earth appear and become solid; let it be done. Thus they spoke. Let there be light, let there be dawn in the sky and on the earth! There shall be neither glory nor grandeur in our creation and formation until the human being is made, man is formed. [...] First the earth was formed, the mountains and the valleys; the currents of water were divided, the rivulets were running freely between the hills, and the water was separated when the high mountains appeared. Thus was the earth created, when it was formed by the Heart of Heaven, the Heart of Earth, as they are called who first made it fruitful, when the sky was in suspense, and the earth was submerged in the water."

The Maya gods Q'uq'umatz (the Maya version of Quetzalcoatl) and Tepeu set about creating the Earth and all its features, finally raising the sky overhead (the Sun came later). The various features of the earth are raised from sea through the conversation between the deities. The two gods then populated the Earth with all manner of animals whom they hoped would worship them, but when the animals proved unable to speak and thus worship the gods, the deities condemned them to be food for higher beings. The two gods next fashioned the first humans from mud, hoping their creation would worship them, but the mud-men dissolved before their eyes and were also unable to worship their creators. For the third attempt at creating worshippers, the tow deities enlisted the skills of the ancestral diviners Xpiyacoc and Xmucane to craft the next iteration of humans. The artisans chose wood as their medium, and though the wooden men reproduced rapidly and populated the Earth, they soon forgot their creators and refused to worship them. The gods grew tired of their ungrateful charges and sent a great flood and a rain of pitch upon them, eventually turning their cooking utensils and dogs against them.

The fourth and final attempt at creating a worshipful populace was comprised of a group of the four founders of the Quiché Maya royal lineages made from maize. The maize men surpassed the expectations of the gods; they praised them as they desired but also worried the gods with their behavior. As a result, the gods enabled them only to see what was nearby. The maize version of humans eventually established the royal lineages of the Quiché and learned to properly worship their gods, as depicted in the *Popol Vuh*:

"This the Forefathers did, Tepeu and Gucumatz, as they were called. After that they began to talk about the creation and the making of our first mother and father; of yellow corn and of white corn they made their flesh; of cornmeal dough they made the arms and the legs of man. Only dough of corn meal went into the flesh of our first fathers, the four men, who were created. [...] And as they had the appearance of men, they were men; they talked, conversed, saw and heard, walked, grasped things; they were good and handsome men, and their figure was the figure of a man."

All these events occurred before the creation of the "true" sun and parallel a common Native American idea that there were several versions of humans that had been created before the current iteration.

The narrative then relates the story of two brothers, Hun Hunahpu and Vucub Hunahpu, who were very skilled "ball-game" players. In most Maya cities that have been excavated, there is at least one ball court, indicating the central importance of the game now referred to as pok-ta-pok. The long rectangular structures with sloping or vertical walls along the sides were the sites of a game in which two teams of 2-7 people moved a rubber ball by hitting it with the body without the use of hands or feet. The most effective method of directing the ball was through the use of the hips. The goal was to pass the ball through a vertical circular ring attached to the long wall of the court. The game was played on courts of various sizes and design, many with boundaries outlined by tall walls and shaped like the English capital letter "I." Protective gear shielded players from the impact of the heavy ball which varied in size from four to twelve inches in diameter and could weigh as much as seven pounds.

This game or a variant of it was important in several Mesoamerican cultures, but based on the archeological evidence the Maya considered it to be a central feature in their urban life. Sculpture associated with ball courts suggest that the game concluded with ritual human sacrifice, presumably captives, although some have suggested that the losing team or the captain of the team were treated to sacrificial execution. This procedure makes sense in the light of the theory that the game was a way of settling municipal grievances or inter-city wars. If the game was merely played for the sake of entertainment and competition, a ritual sacrifice of the losers would have been a rather severe method of improving the quality of play.

The Mesoamerican ballgame was played throughout all levels of society, from "sand lot" games to competitions with sacrificial consequences, occurring between the elites. Such games had grave consequences, and again depending on the variation, the losing team might be sacrificed to the gods. According to the *Popol Vuh*, Hun Hunahpu and Vucub Hunahpu were such skilled players and played so often that the noise of their games disturbed the lords of Xibalba (the Maya Underworld). The brothers were commanded to come to Xibalba to play a game, and guide owls were sent from Xibalba to guide the brothers to the underworld ball court. Hun Hunahpu and Vucub Hunahpu failed test after test from the death gods of Xibalba and were sacrificed the day after they arrived in the underworld. Hun Hunahpu's head was removed and mounted in a calabash tree as though in a *tzompantli* (skull rack), where the skulls of sacrificial victims were collected and displayed. The brothers' bodies were buried under the ball court.

"'Well. Today shall be the end of your days. Now you shall die. You shall be destroyed, we will break you into pieces and here your faces will stay hidden. You shall be sacrificed,' said Hun-Camé and Vucub-Camé.

They sacrificed them immediately and buried them in the Pucbal-Chah, as it was called. Before burying them, they cut off the head of Hun-Hunahpú and buried the older brother together with the younger brother.

'Take the head and put it in that tree which is planted on the road,' said Hun-Camé and Vucub-Camé. And having put the head in the tree, instantly the tree, which had never borne fruit before the head of Hun-Hunahpú was placed among its branches, was covered with fruit. And this calabash tree, it is said, is the one which we now call the head of Hun-Hunahpú."

When she heard that Hun Hunahpu's head was mounted in the tree, a young Xibalba goddess named Xquic went to visit the odd fruit, and the goddess was impregnated when Hun Hunahpu spat into her hand. Now pregnant with the twins Hunahpu and Xbalanque, the goddess was driven from the underworld by the lords there and was led by an owl to live with Hun Hunahpu's mother. The older woman tested Xquic before allowing her to move in with her and complete her pregnancy.

Hun Hunahpu had fathered an earlier pair of twins, Hun Batz and Hun Chuen, who had become accomplished artists and musicians, and the older twins often teased and took advantage of their younger brothers. Eventually, Hunahpu and Xbalanque grew old enough to outsmart their older brothers and lured them into trees where they were transformed into monkeys because they could not climb down. In addition, the younger twins convinced their older siblings to let their loin cloths trail behind them, which eventually became their tails. The older twins were then transformed into the twin Monkey gods, patrons of writing and other arts. The two gods can be distinguished by their names. Batz is the Quiché word for howler monkey, while Chuen is the word for spider monkey. The two gods are considered gifted, industrious, and licentious.

The Popol Vuh offers an anecdote detailing how the twins succeeded in casting down Vucub Caquix, who set himself up as a false sun supported by his two sons.

"'I shall now be great above all the beings created and formed. I am the sun, the light, the moon,' he exclaimed. 'Great is my splendor. Because of me men shall walk and conquer. For my eyes are of silver, bright, resplendent as precious stones, as emeralds; my teeth shine like perfect stones, like the face of the sky. My nose shines afar like the moon, my throne is of silver, and the face of the earth is lighted when I pass before my throne.'

'So, then, I am the sun, I am the moon, for all mankind. So shall it be, because I can see very far.' So Vucub-Caquix spoke. But he was not really the sun; he was only vainglorious of his feathers and his riches. And he could see only as far as the horizon, and he could not see over all the world.

The face of the sun had not yet appeared, nor that of the moon, nor the stars, and it had not dawned. Therefore, Vucub-Caquix became as vain as though he were the sun and the moon, because the light of the sun and the moon had not yet shown itself. His only ambition was to exalt himself and to dominate. And all this happened when the flood came because of the wooden people."

However, having grown into accomplished blowgunners, the twins shot out the jeweled teeth of Vucub-Caquix and convinced him to accept ground corn as a replacement. Deprived of the jewels that provided his radiance and unable to eat, Vucub Caquix was soon defeated. His sons fell shortly afterwards.

Fearing that her grandsons would fall to the same fate as her sons, the twins' grandmother hid their father's ball game equipment from them, but they soon outwitted her and began playing the ball game, becoming more skilled than their father had been. Just as their father and uncle had, Hunahpu and Xbalanque attracted the attention of the lords of Xibalba who demanded that the young heroes travel to the underworld and play the ball game, but this time the Hero Twins were more successful in the underworld than their father had been, and they were able to use a mosquito to bite each of the death gods in sequence, thus revealing their names (a key to defeating them). Every day, the twins played the ball game against the Xibalba lords, and each evening they were ordered to report to a different house to be tested. Through their ingenuity, they were able to pass the underworld tests; for example, when told to keep cigars lit all night, they caught fireflies and placed them on the ends of them. When the lords of Xibalba told the Twins to provide cut flowers, they summoned cutter ants which harvested the Xibalban flowers for them. Sent to a "cold" house, the Twins drove away the cold; sent to the jaguar house, they appeased the cat with the flesh of other animals. The fire in the "fire" house could not consume them, but despite sleeping inside their blowguns, Hunahpu's head was sliced off by a killer bat in the "bat" house. Xbalanque summoned animals to help him, and they fashioned a head for Hunahpu from a pumpkin.

When the twins arrived at the ball court for the daily game, the lords of Xibalba introduced Hunahpu's head as the game ball. At the start of the game, Xbalanque struck the ball and drove it out of the court. Simultaneously, a rabbit bounded away, pretending to be the lost ball and leading the death gods away from Hunahpu's head. Xbalanque found his brother's head and restored it to his body, but the two were then defeated and roasted in an oven. Their bones were ground into powder and dumped into the river.

Five days later, the Twins emerged from the river, first as catfish, then transforming into humans and disguising themselves as traveling magicians and performers. The Twins were soon summoned to the Xibalban court, where they danced and sacrificed and revived a dog and a human. Xbalanque then sacrificed and revived Hunahpu. Seeing this, the lords of Xibalba begged to be sacrificed themselves, to which the Twins readily agreed. The Hero Twins sacrificed the death gods but did not revive them. They exhumed the bodies of Hun Hunahpu and Vucub Hunahpu and after reviving them, walked into the sky to reign over it as the sun and the moon.

Returning to the maize humans introduced earlier in the narrative, the *Popol Vuh* then recounts the journey of the four founders of the Quiché Royal lineages to Tulan Zuyua (a region of mountains and caves), where they retrieved the slain gods and carried them in bundles on their backs. Balam Quetzal carried the remains of the god Tohil, who agreed to give men the gift of fire after human sacrifice dedicated to him begins. When the Quiché royals agreed and began human sacrifice, the true sun rose, and in closing, the *Popol Vuh* lists the 14 generations of Ahaus from Balam Quetzal to the generation of the original, Quiché writer in the mid-16th century.

Although it is probable that some of the original Paleoindian inhabitants of the Americas migrated from northeastern Asia across the Bering Land Bridge, there is little direct evidence to suggest an Asian lineage for Mesoamerican religious beliefs. Evidence of complex religious behavior (ceremonial burials) dating between 5000 and 6000 B.C. has been found in highland southern Mexico, and a possible ancient ball court has been found in the same region. The significance of the Mesoamerican ball game to religious practice is direct, in that the game figures prominently in the *Popol Vuh*. The foundational narrative also introduces a number of tropes that are central to both Maya civilization and religion, which are inextricably intertwined. The narrative introduces the Mesoamerican ball game, which is made all the more significant because the Maya saw in it the metaphorical machinations of the universe; a player who was unprepared and off balance might be killed by the ball. The game was life and death at both real and spiritual levels, and eventually, it became a regular ritual practice within the large, Maya urban centers, providing both entertainment and regular, sacrificial victims.

The Popol Vuh also demonstrates the importance of the concept of human sacrifice, a practice central to many Mesoamerican civilizations. When the Hero Twins sacrifice and then revive humans, the lords of Xibalba beg to be sacrificed and the prototypical humans trick their way out of a spiritually tight spot. But later the founders of the Quiché Royal lineages agree to conduct human sacrifice and thus gain the technology of fire and spark the rising of the true sun.

Furthermore, fundamental Maya religious imagery depicting a close association to the natural world appears in the *Popol Vuh*. Owls appear playing pivotal roles, and for the Maya owls were associated with caves, which were in turn considered portals to the underworld. First, the owl serves the lords of Xibalba and guides the first pair of brothers into the underworld. The second appearance of an owl has an owl leading the mother of the Hero Twins out of the underworld and to Hun Hunahpu's mother.

Regarding caves, the Quiché Royals journeyed to a region of caves to collect the remains of the gods of the underworld. By serving as portals or gateways to the underworld, caves and the mountains where they often occur are considered the places where the veil between the spiritual and physical realms in thinnest.

The appearance of cultivated plants (maize and calabash) in association with reproduction and renewal illustrate Maya beliefs regarding their agricultural technologies. The pivotal role of maize as a literal building block of humanity demonstrates the Maya understanding of the value of the technology associated with the cultivation of maize, while the appearance of the calabash tree (*Crescentia*) represents both medicinal and practical uses of cultivated plants. Calabash can be harvested young and used as a vegetable or allowed to mature and then dried and made into containers. One variety's pulp is used medicinally for respiratory problems. In some artistic depictions, Hun Hunahpu's head is depicted as an ear of corn, though the narrative states he was in a calabash tree, indicating its vital importance as a sustaining and renewing food source. The centrality of maize cultivation to Maya religious thought is further demonstrated by the Maya predilection for viewing human life and death in terms associated with the life-cycle of the maize plant.

Chapter 6: The Concept of Death

Among Mesoamericans, life and death were closely related and often deeply integrated, and the two conditions were perceived to exist in an opposition that was at once dynamic and complementary. Described later by the Aztecs as the state of *nepantla*, life and death were viewed by the indigenous people of Mesoamerica as yet another example of the "back and forth" fluctuations common to human life.

Sometimes simplistically described as a borderland or liminal place, nepantla is a far more nuanced term and concept. For Mesoamericans there were no "disasters"; life only happened, and the way of that happening was by this back-and-forth, give-and-take model. Because death, killing, and sacrifice were necessary for life and required for nourishment, their necessity was understood and accepted.

The introduction of ancestor worship and rebirth into the equation further clouds modern potential for understanding Maya conceptions of death. Deceased ancestors were not buried apart from their families; rather, they were often buried beneath the floor of the family home. In that way, ancestors were included in daily life and were kept apprised of family milestones. Also, ancestors could influence their living descendants or act as intermediaries between the living and the gods. Unhappy or dishonored ancestors could even inflict diseases from the underworld, seen as the source for illness.

Thus, major festivals honored the deceased, and the living sought to commune with them by presenting offerings of food and flowers. This reverence, and attempts to appease departed loved ones, is another example of a ritual which survived the conquest and became an accepted, albeit folk-Catholic, tradition. Originally conducted during late summer (August), post-conquest iterations of the celebrations gradually migrated through the calendar until they coincided with the Catholic celebrations of All Saints' Day and All Souls' Day. Commonly known as the Day of the Dead, this Mesoamerican ancestor-honoring ritual still occurs throughout Latin America, the southwestern part of the United States, and anywhere that Latinos with ancestral ties to Mesoamerica live. The physical genuineness of the gifts presented at Day of the Dead shrines, food, drinks, and flowers, mimics the both the content and the idea behind the funeral goods often found in internments of Maya elites.

Like the ancient Egyptians, the Maya believed that the afterlife was a place where the real needs of daily life (like food and money) were necessary, so wealthy Maya elites were buried with an elaborate assortment of funerary goods. Among the goods elites carried with them into death were containers of a cacao-based drink, attendants, dogs, and often large amounts of jade, cloth, and rope. Even poor Maya were buried with a jade bead in their mouths as a bit of currency that they might need in the afterlife.

For the Egyptians, the weight of their deeds in life was measured in the underworld on a scale, while the Maya viewed the voyage of death into the underworld as a series of tests the decedent must overcome. For the Maya, the journey into the afterlife began with crossing over still waters, often depicted artistically by a canoe trip. After this initial voyage, the voyager traveled through various levels of the underworld, depicted in the *Popol Vuh* as the "houses" where the Hero Twins were tested. In order to overcome death, Maya had to outwit the death gods and pass the tests they encountered during their journeys through Xibalba. Though the gods of death were sometimes treated with derision because they were often outsmarted by men, they were also widely feared and considered ruthless and cunning. Their fallibility offered humans hope that they might negotiate the trials of the underworld and ultimately overcome them.

The underworld in Maya religion is also associated with foul smells, and often these levels were steaming hot scenes of decay and decomposition where the gods of death lived. The Maya equivalent of the Aztec god of the underworld, Mictlantecuhtli, is referred to as *cizin* or "the flatulent one" in the Madrid Codex (one of the four surviving Maya codices), and Lacondon and Yucatec Maya still refer to the death god as *Cizin* (kee-ZEEN). This god is often depicted as a skeletal figured adorned with strips of paper, a common gift to the dead and when blood soaked, a part of the autosacrificial rituals performed by Maya elites. The depiction of death gods is often animated and suggests a familiarity that borders on affection, as though the certainty of death has rendered the god's existence and powers moot.

Mayan depiction of Cizin

Chapter 7: Human Sacrifice

Like most Mesoamerican civilizations, the Maya practiced human sacrifice as an essential ritual in their religious, political, and civic lives. Because the Maya left writings, it is known that Ahaus claimed sacrificial victims that they had either personally sacrificed or had personally captured in battle. Like their Roman counterparts, victorious Maya warriors and Ahaus sometimes led their captives through their cities, strapped to scaffolding and displayed for all to see. Maya artistic depictions of human sacrifice show captives sacrificed by decapitation, sometimes after torture. Victims might be burnt, scalped, or disemboweled. Some were trussed into mock imitations of the ball from the Mesoamerican ball game and bounced. Others were utilized in other more specific sacrificial rituals and were dressed as deer and then sacrificed during a *scapedeer* ritual.

The relative ranking of sacrificial captives was very important to Maya elites, and warriors always strived to capture victims that were members of the enemy elite or high-ranking members of one of the various knight orders (like the Jaguar or Eagle). Enemy lords were most desirable, and the ranking of enemies captured added to a Maya lord's prestige, political power, and tribute. Artistic examples of sacrificial scenes can often be found on the risers of steps leading to the site of sacrifice, atop sacrificial structures as though to remind to victim what awaited him/her at the top of the temple.

While not as central to life as it was to the Aztecs, human sacrifice was important enough and gruesome enough among the Maya to disgust the Spanish, who were hardly averse to bloodshed. One of the Spanish clergy, De Landa, wrote about Maya sacrifice, "After the people had been thus instructed in religion, and the youths benefitted as we have said, they were perverted by their priests and chiefs to return to their idolatry; this they did, making sacrifices not only by incense, but also of human blood. Upon this the friars held an Inquisition, calling upon the Alcalde Mayor for aid; they held trials and celebrated an Auto, putting many on scaffolds, capped, shorn and beaten, and some in the penitential robes for a time. Some of the Indians out of grief, and deluded by the devil, hung themselves; but generally they all showed much repentance and readiness to be good Christians."

However, not all forms of blood sacrifice ended in a violent and gruesome death for the victim. At Palenque (in present-day Chiapas, Mexico), a 25 year old woman sealed herself into a tomb with a de-fleshed skeleton using plaster to seal the exit. She left her handprints in the plaster and sat in a corner, awaiting her own death. In another similarity between Maya and ancient Egyptian burial customs, servants were sometimes buried with elites, presumably because they would be needed in the afterlife.

For Maya elites, servants were just another component in funeral goods, but for the Maya sacrificial rituals, sometimes the blood of lords and ladies was required. Both men and women among the Maya elites practiced ritual bloodletting; for example, men often pierced their genitals with maguey or stingray spines, and graphic scenes of this form of sacrifice were captured by Maya artists and recorded on numerous painted pots dating from the Classic Period. Alternatively, perhaps depending upon the particular ritual, men might draw blood from their pierced earlobes or draw a spiked cord through their tongues. Meanwhile, female elites drew blood from their earlobes or via the aforementioned spiked cord in a similar fashion. Recent artistic evidence, including the depiction of a female Maya with a sacred, stingray-spine perforator over her genital area, may indicate that female Maya elites also pierced their genitals and drew sacrificial blood.

Sculpture of a Maya blood sacrifice. King "Shield Jaguar" is shown holding a torch, while Queen "Lady Xoc" draws a barbed rope through her pierced tongue.

Before these sacrificial events, participants engaged in cleansing rituals such as fasting and abstinence to purify themselves before offering their blood to the gods. The participants may have then made offerings of food, ornaments, and other valuables. Maya elites engaged in ritual bloodletting with the goal of entering a "vision quest" state and communing with their ancestors or opening the portal to the underworld. The blood was collected on slips of bark paper and burned as an offering to the god or gods toward which the sacrifice was dedicated. In the smoke from the burned sacrificial blood, Maya elites believed they could communicate with their ancestors, and such scenes have been depicted in famous carvings at the ancient Maya city of

Yaxchilan.

Closely tied to this is the concept that ancestors were reborn in their descendants and that special sacrifices allowed the descendant to call forth specific ancestor to be reborn into specific children. This involved among the most appalling type of sacrifice committed by any ancient peoples, the sacrifice of infants. The specific rituals invoked using infant sacrifices were called *k'ex* or "substitution" by the Maya. In essence, the sacrificial victim stands in proxy for the one conducting (or benefitting from) the ritual. The infant in this case is sacrificed to the Lords of Xibalba in exchange for the release of an ancestor for rebirth. One archaeological dig in Belize turned up the corpses of 5 children, ranging in age from infancy to 8 years old, that demonstrated the practice of child sacrifice was normal.

A similar version of this "substitution" ritual was used during accession rituals. Ideally, a high-ranking sacrificial (another Maya lord) served as the sacrificial victim during the accession of the new Ahau. Victims were trussed in scaffoldings and sacrificed, after which the new Ahau took their place and emerged from the bindings on the scaffold as though reborn.

The importance of the natural world and its processes are demonstrated by the personal bloodletting conducted by the elites. Such blood was sacred to the maize gods, and because maize cannot complete its life-cycle without the assistance of humans, the elites and their blood were vital to the continual rebirth and regeneration of Maya society. Ahaus sometimes depicted themselves as a maize god on stelae, evoking both the idea of the Ahau as vital to the rebirth of the people and to perpetuate the belief in ancestor rebirth (through the smoke portal described above). At Copan (in present-day Honduras), the Ahau Waxaklahun-Ubah-K'awil had himself depicted thus, as well as on a second very detailed stela showing him with perforators (the spines used to draw blood) illustrated as personified gods above his head and on his loincloth. In this case, the Ahau's likeness may have been prophetic; he was captured about a year after the commissioned stela was completed and sacrificed by K'ak'-Tiliw, the Ahau of Quirigua. Illustrations depicting this form of blood sacrifice often adorned temples, and the individuals were usually shown in the act of autosacrificial bloodletting and with the necessary accouterments.

This aspect of Maya religious practice lasted at least into the colonial period, as Spanish colonial sources have described Maya engaged in the practice. However, the Spanish Catholic priests sought to actively eradicate indigenous religious practices among the subjugated Maya, especially a practice they considered so gruesome and a form of apostasy. Indigenous religious practitioners who were found engaged in their traditional religious activity were whipped, beaten, stretched on the rack, scalded with boiling water, and tortured in a myriad of ways.

Though the existence of cannibalism among the Maya has been debated in the past, it is clear that it occurred throughout Mesoamerica to varying degrees. Some have asserted that it did not occur among the Maya, but others note that in the period just prior to the Spanish conquest, human flesh composed a major component of the Aztec diet. Not all of these reports can be attributed to pre-existing European biases either, as early colonial indigenous documents show significant evidence of cannibalism.

Regardless, consuming human flesh was neither common nor a behavior undertaken flippantly. For Mesoamericans, ritual cannibalism was an act imbued with religious significance. Diego de Landa, a Catholic Bishop who worked among the Maya during the colonial period, writes that Yucatec Maya (in the lowlands of present-day Yucatan, Mexico) considered the flesh of human sacrificial victims to be a sacred food. This conception of sacrificial victims as sacred food source extends to most (if not all) Mesoamerican civilizations and played a key role in religious rituals. Cannibalism was a central factor in rituals which involved deity impersonation, when priests or Ahau would take on the persona of specific gods. Because the gods fed on human flesh—purified and rendered divine by the sacrificial process—the impersonator effectively mimicked the gods by consuming divinity.

Chapter 8: Cosmology

In 2012, much of the interest in the Maya is a result of their calendar, particularly the fact that it ends on December 21, 2012. While many incorrectly presume that the Maya were predicting the world to end on that date, it is not a coincidence that their calendar ended on the winter solstice. The Maya developed a sophisticated method of calculating and creating a calendar that is astonishing even by today's standards, and their advancements in applied mathematics not only has intrigued archaeologists but has been incorporated into the beliefs of New Agers and modern apocalyptic doomsayers. In the history of arithmetic, their use of zero stands as a milestone of great significance, which placed them ahead of contemporary Europeans. In Europe, this essential concept was not part of the canon of calculation until the Renaissance.

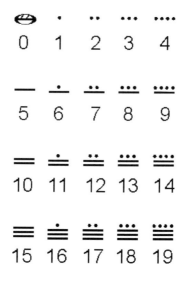

Mayan numerology

   The Maya numerical system was based on units of 20. To represent the numerals 1 to 4 they used dots. Five was written with a horizontal bar and 6 was a bar with a dot above. Up to 19, the Maya were able to use a system of dots and bars. For example three bars and a dot signified 16. The zero was represented by a shell. The written number system not only allowed calculation of items of trade but also permitted the calculations necessary in order to record time, as well as for the creation of a calendar.

   The Maya used two calendars. One was a 260 day ritual calendar with twelve 20 day cycles. They also used a 365 solar count calendar which consisted of eighteen months of 20 days, and five uncategorized days at the end of the year. While this calendrical system was common in Mesoamerican cultures, the Maya were unique in the creation of what is called the Long Count. They established a zero date which has been correlated with the West's Gregorian calendar to stand for August 11, 3114 B.C. Time was measured from this starting date in five units, a *baktun* of 144,000 days, a *katun* of 7,200 days, a *tun* of 360 days, a *uinal* of 20 days, and a *kin* of 1 day. Dates were written with a point between each unit so that a date from year zero would be so many *baktuns* followed by a dot, then so many *katuns* followed by a dot, so many *tuns* and so on. Using this Long Count method of indicating dates, the Maya recorded in inscriptions and on freestanding commemorative relief carved stones (stelae) the actual date of important events, such as the accession of a king or a military victory. In Maya civilization time was an essential concept. The past, the present and the future were clearly related and all kinds of social activities could be managed in a world organized by time.

For day to day purposes the Maya used the ritual calendar of twelve 20 day cycles. Each month was given a name and astrologers using the celestial bodies could plot the most auspicious time for such activities as planting or waging war. A priest scribe, *ak k'u hun* ("servant of the sun"), managed the connection between astronomy and the calendar, and as keeper of the time he was also the curator of the genealogies of kings and nobles.

With its 225 day orbit around the sun and its phases, Venus was one focus of astronomical observation from observatories like the one at Chichén Itzá. To the Maya, the cyclical disappearance of Venus connected the planet with the underworld. The appearance of Venus as the morning star and evening star were predicted by Maya astronomers with an accuracy of one day in 6,000 years. The observatory at Chichén Itzá (the Coracol) was built primarily for the observation of Venus, and the three doors to the inner chamber line up with precisely with the position in the western sky where Venus can be seen as the evening star. Evidence of the importance of astronomical prediction in Maya society is found in two of the surviving Maya manuscripts. The Grolier Codex, which was written around 1230 A.D., and the Dresden Codex, written just before the Spanish conquest, have tables for the plotting of the phases of Venus, Mars, and solar eclipses.

Mesoamerican cosmology also closely associated colors with specific directions. The ancient Maya were most specific in this regard and created certain distinct glyphs for the colors red, black, white, and yellow, each of which corresponded to one of the cardinal directions. Red was associated with the east, black with the west; white was associated with the north and yellow with the south. The glyph and color green signified the "center." While there are conflicting accounts regarding the identification of specific colors with certain cardinal directions, most Mesoamerican civilization agreed in associating the color white with the north and yellow with the south. For the Maya, the colors represented not only directional visions but also referred to orientation and positionality. By the early Classic period, written evidence indicates the clear creation and establishment of these colors and their directional associations were uniformly recognized across Mesoamerica.

Chapter 9: Deities

Maya deities existed in a large pantheon of about 165 gods, representing various aspects, cycles, and patterns. Mayan gods came in all ages, shapes, and sizes, including, young, old, or combined characteristics or plant *and* animal characteristics simultaneously. The Greek conception of Zeus and the other Olympian gods is quite similar to descriptions of Maya deities in their early mythology, who acted much like humans. Maya gods were born, grew through stages of life, endured rites of passage, went through transformations, died, and were often reborn. The early models of the Maya gods established cornfields and planted and harvested crops.

Maya deities could manifest themselves in any number of forms that reflected their spheres of influence and control. Gods might take the forms of animals, plants, natural geological formations, and weather events like wind, fire, thunder, or lightning. The deities often reflected multiple aspects and are sometimes depicted in carvings in multiple versions, each possessing a unique aspect.

Like Maya lords of the Classic Period, the Maya gods of legend performed divinations, conducted business, formed alliances, fought wars, and intermarried. This behavior served a dual purpose as a model for appropriate human behavior and provided the rationale for and justification of activities conducted by Maya elites, societal hierarchies, religious rituals, and political structures. Maya lords often arrayed themselves in the accoutrements of the god being honored by wearing facemasks and costumes and also assuming the traits and behaviors of the deity. The gods also possessed *way'ob* (WY-ohb, *way* is the singular version), or spirit animals into which they can transform at will, a common Native American and animistic religious belief. The idea that gods (and humans) possess these spirit/animal companions illustrates a central belief among the Maya regarding the duality of the soul. The *way* serves as a spiritual protector and supernatural guardian, and the baby and the *way's* fates were linked so that what happened to one also affected the other, whether good or bad. Eventually, these seminal gods searched for maize (both yellow and white) and fashioned humans from it, and humans held maize sacred as a result.

Appropriately, Maize itself was considered a god and was often depicted as multiple handsome young faces forming multiple ears of maize. The faces are shown with flowing locks of corn silk forming hair and bright green leaves moving like human limbs. The Maize god was also androgynous, referred to by Maya as a "mother-father" because it possessed aspects of both genders. Depending upon the season in which the god is depicted, the Maize god will appear differently. Early in the season, he appears as a young man, but during the harvest he is decapitated (a common form of Maya human sacrifice) and his severed head appears on a platter as a ritual offering. Later in the Fall, he is ground into *masa* (corn meal dough) and formed into tamales and tortillas, providing sustenance for humans. The humans eventually return a few of the seeds of the Maize god to the ground, where he shortly emerges, reborn again as a young handsome man.

Classic Period depiction of Itzamna

Colonial Yucatec Maya accounts describe Itzamna as the chief god among the Maya deities, and he is often addressed with the title of *ahaulil*, or "lord." Classic Period vessels depicted Itzamna seated in a throne above and ruling over lesser gods. The Postclassic Yucatec Maya tradition held that he was the first priest and the inventor of writing. During the Maya month Uo, priests brought their own codex-books and presented them to an image of the deity. During the Late Classic, Itzamna was often portrayed as a scribe, and at the site of Xcalumkin he bears the moniker "He of the Writing."

Also associated with the healing arts, Itzamna was worshipped as the god of medicine during the Yucatec month Zip. Part of the deity's name, *itzam*, refers to a caiman (a type of crocodile native to Mesoamerica) and illustrates his association with water and land, as the god who set the throne stone in the cosmic hearth. He is even associated with the flood that destroyed one version of creation.

Along with Itzamna, and forming another Maya duality, Ix Chel personified one of the "grandparents" of the *Popol Vuh*, Xpiyacoc and Xmucane. The pair were considered deities related to medicine, and priests and healers called upon them while praying for their patients. Her name can be roughly translated as "Lady Rainbow," and she was an iconic Maya female, being the first weaver, cotton spinner, mother, and midwife. Considered a major goddess by the time of the Spanish conquest, Ix Chel was the patroness of childbirth, pregnancy, divination, midwifery, and fertility. From throughout the Yucatecan lowlands, Maya women made long and dangerous pilgrimages to her shrines on the islands of Cozumel and Isla Mujeres.

Despite this wide devotion, none of her statues or sculptures on those islands have survived. She is called *Chac Chel* in the Dresden Codex, one of the four surviving Maya codices, and therein she is portrayed in a different aspect. She appears as an aging crone with snakes for hair, who sometimes has jaguar claws and cat eyes and might be dressed in a blouse bearing a "skull and crossbones" pattern.

Depiction of Ix Chel in the Dresden Codex

Among the oldest of the formally worshipped Maya gods, Chaac is the god of rain and lightning. His images appear in Pre-Classic Maya sites, where he appears arrayed as a fisherman, casting a net and carrying his catch in a creel on his back. During the Classic Period, Chaac is often portrayed as a quasi-reptilian figure, replete with a blunt snout, body scales, and catfish-like whiskers. He sometimes also bears a *spondylus* shell, a female symbol (the shell itself is red and resembles a vagina) illustrating one of his alternate aspects. By the Postclassic Period, he appears more human in form but is often depicted with a long nose and tends to bear more iconography related to his powers of lightning (a stone axe or a serpent). Chaac is credited with opening the great rock that contained the original maize, and this myth has been depicted in sculpture for over 1,000 years. The rain and lightning god remains one of the few classic gods still regularly worshipped by modern Maya.

Urn depicting Chaac dating from the 12th-14th centuries.

Known alternately as Manikin Scepter and the Flare god, K'awiil is also closely associated with the Aztec god Tezcatlipoca. This god is both the statue portraying him and the spirit of that statue; he has multiple different forms and aspects. The god is portrayed with a cigar, axe blade, or torch-holder penetrating an obsidian mirror on his forehead and has animalistic facial features. His body is often infantile, but one of his legs is usually formed into a snake-like *way* (spirit guardian). He is considered a *Patron God* of Copan. His Aztec version, Tezcatlipoca's name refers to a "smoking mirror" which refers both to an obsidian mirror and the surface of the Earth itself. The Aztec version is closely tied to Mesoamerican creation myths and *Tollan* (the land of mountains and caves), and he is often portrayed as an analog for the Hero Twins and described as outwitting other gods, especially Quetzalcoatl.

Depiction of K'awiil

Like Chaac, Tezcatlipoca's image appears throughout Mesoamerica, in all regional historical periods. Both K'awil and Tezcatlipoca are closely associated with the supreme office of leadership among Mesoamerican peoples, however, the two gods are not equivalent. K'awiil has distinctive serpent like qualities, while Tezcatlipoca is clearly associated with jaguar characteristics.

Each Maya (and Mesoamerican) city-state maintained its own titular gods, and it is presumed these gods were secured in sacred bundles maintained in each city-state. Ethnographies indicate that patron gods for the Quiché and Kaqchikel Maya were awarded to them in Tollan (the sacred place), and the Maya in those city-states closely guarded their gods. K'awiil, for example, was one of the patron gods of Palenque. However, despite being kept in sacred places, these gods could be captured or destroyed during battle. Such an event was catastrophic for the city-state that lost its patron because its capture or destruction invalidated its supernatural protective shield.

The death god (Cizin among the Yucatec and Lacondon Maya) is often ornamented with bell-shaped decorations that serve to warn humans of his approach. Ah Pukuh's name refers to demon or devil, and he is also known as Yum Kimil. He is known as the god of war and violent death, and he rules over Mitnal (Aztec-Mictlan). He may be depicted as a skeletal figure with a bloated belly (indicating worm infestation or the decay of a corpse), and dogs or Owls are his close associates because dogs allegedly know their way through the underworld and owls are associated with caves and served as guides in the *Popol Vuh*.

This god appears in many guises, nearly as many as his namesake suggests, and may appear as a skeletal figure, adorned with paper strips, dancing and quite similar to the common skeleton figure seen in Day of the Dead celebrations. His name likely refers to the lord of the underworld in lord of the underworld in the Tzeltal, Tzotzil, and Tojolabal Maya languages.

Q'uq'umatz is the Maya version of the widely known Mesoamerican god Quetzalcoatl (also Kukulcan), whose name literally means "feathered serpent." This god is among the most wide-spread Mesoamerican images or ideas, and imagery related to Q'uq'umatz is found as far north as the modern Pueblo peoples of the U.S. Southwest. The serpent is specifically a rattlesnake, while the bird is the plumed quetzal (*Pharomachrus mocinno*). Maya languages render the terms for *snake* and *sky* identically, and the god represents in part the everlasting snake in the sky the Maya see. Q'uq'umatz partnered with Teleu and was present during the initial creation of humans, and he is often confused with an actual king of Tula (legendary Tollan) named Ce Acatl Topiltzin Quetzalcoatl, who may have visited Chichen Itza (as Kukulcan) and spawned the Quetzalcoatl legend upon which the Spanish conquistador Hernan Cortés capitalized.

A ball court marker that depicts Q'uq'umatz carrying Tohil across the sky in his jaw

Chapter 10: The Collapse and Resurrection of Maya Culture

Eventually the great Maya cities began to lose their populations, one by one. The collapse came first to the cities of the southern lowlands. For example, building came to a halt and ritual ceremonies were abandoned at Palenque in 799 and Tikal in 879. In the northern lowlands of the Yucatan, the cities of the Puuc hills such as Uxmal were abandoned starting around 920, and Chichén Itzá was partially abandoned in 948. The culture of the Maya survived in a disorganized way until it was revived at Mayapán around 1200.

Why Maya cities were abandoned and left to be overgrown by the jungle is a puzzle that intrigues curious people around the world today, especially those who have a penchant for speculating on lost civilizations. Often, conjecture on the cause of the end of the Maya civilization has depended on the preconceptions of the observer. If one were to ask Bishop Landa why the Maya he met and talked to were in such a sorry state he would have said that their condition was a result of their unbaptized state. Some American archaeologists, living in the era of frighteningly bloody mass wars of the 20th century, suggested that the Maya destroyed themselves by constant inter-city warfare. Others writing in the era of the rise of Communism believed that Maya cities collapsed because of class warfare. In the 21st century, a more common theory on the collapse of the Maya is that they were forced by drought, overpopulation and unsustainable agricultural practices to move away from their urban centres. What probably happened was that some or all these social and environmental factors (with the exception of Landa's religious notions) converged in such a way that even the strongest of Maya cities were unable to survive.

As it was, the Maya civilization was already in a serious state of decline when the Europeans arrived in their territory. The Spanish did their best to ensure that the final nail was driven into the Maya coffin, both through the spread of warfare and disease, but the Mayan culture was never completely eradicated.

The Caste War

In the struggle for independence in Mexico, the elite of the Yucatan opted for a federalist model of administration for the new country. In 1838 Yucatecos revolted against the interference of the government in Mexico City and in the years following engaged in armed struggle to defend the virtual independence of the Yucatan. In this struggle they enlisted Maya as cannon fodder and promised them remission of taxes and monies paid to the church. The Yucatec authorities did not honor their agreement and in 1847 Maya troops revolted in Valladolid. Using the weapons that they retained from service in the Yucatec army and weapons supplied by the British through Belize, the Maya insurgents in the Caste War, as it came to be known, almost succeeded taking over the entire Yucatan. On the eve of what would have been a successful siege of Mérida, the Maya soldiers gave up and returned to their fields. Pursued by the Yucatec forces the Maya melted into the jungle and formed communities that exist to this day.

Modern Maya Culture

Most Maya are mainstream Catholics today, but some engage in a sort of "folk Catholicism" that combines traditional Maya religious practices and ideas absorbed and translated into Catholic religious practice. The renewal ritual – carrying the statues of saints through sawdust murals – slides neatly into its place as a ritual procession conducted in association with Catholic Semana Santa or Holy Week and stands as an example of this Maya/Catholic combination. In a society ravaged by wave after wave of epidemic, exact religious knowledge likely faded with passing generations, and in a sense the oral religious traditions and legends passed down among shell-shocked survivors seems like a believable survival strategy. In an effort to save any aspect of their previously vibrant religious culture, Maya practitioners sought to embed their own practices within the colonizing faith.

In essence, Maya survivors co-opted the Catholic religious hegemony by deliberately associating and embedding indigenous religious traditions and practices into colonial Catholic ritual. As demonstrated by the existence of numerous regional saints with quirky traditional beliefs and folk practices, the Catholic Church seems open to the adoption of indigenous religious practices in the greater interest of converting the population. This openness to the influences of subjugated people has allowed aspects of Maya religious life to survive into the modern era.

There are an estimated 20,000 Maya living in southern California alone, and while most are Catholic, some blend indigenous and Catholic religious beliefs into their version of "Maya Spirituality." These believers blend Christian and Maya beliefs into a faith that includes deference and appreciation for the natural world, meditation, ceremonial dance, and indigenous rituals. Many of these Maya are Guatemalan refugees and their children, who came to the United States after fleeing the decades-long Guatemalan Civil War. Unfortunately, Maya remaining in Guatemala do not enjoy the freedoms of those in the United States, and the burgeoning Guatemalan Evangelical Christian movement is very resistant to a resurgence of traditional Maya religious beliefs.

If one accepts the premise that language is the core of culture, then the Maya culture is alive and well in Mexico and Central America. Some 6 million people in the region speak in one of the Mayan group of languages, and many still adhere to a system of beliefs that combines ancient Mayan religion and Catholicism. Moreover, there is a rich tradition of post-colonial literature in the Mayan language written in Latin script.

Given the world's strong and ongoing interest in the Maya, it seems certain that the culture and legacy of the Maya will never go extinct.

Printed in Great Britain
by Amazon

ISBN 9781493590780

90000